The Desert Speaks to the Dreamer

poems by

Deborah Barrett

Finishing Line Press
Georgetown, Kentucky

The Desert Speaks to the Dreamer

Copyright © 2019 by Deborah Barrett
ISBN 978-1-63534-924-5 First Edition
All rights reserved under International and Pan-American Copyright Conventions.
No part of this book may be reproduced in any manner whatsoever without written
permission from the publisher, except in the case of brief quotations embodied in
critical articles and reviews.

ACKNOWLEDGMENTS

Thanks to my workshop teachers and fellow poets at Stanford and at Bread Loaf for the tutelage and encouragement.

Publisher: Leah Maines
Editor: Christen Kincaid
Cover Art: Deborah Barrett
Author Photo: Deborah Barrett
Cover Design: Leah Huete

Printed in the USA on acid-free paper.
Order online: www.finishinglinepress.com
also available on amazon.com

Author inquiries and mail orders:
Finishing Line Press
P. O. Box 1626
Georgetown, Kentucky 40324
U. S. A.

Table of Contents

The Desert Speaks to the Dreamer 1

To Calliope 2

Darkness Lifting 3

The Greens of Acadia 4

Loss 5

Death Waits 6

Professor Lost 7

The Last Word: A Sestina 8

The Last Great Auk 10

The Lessons of Hurricanes 11

My Life on the Curb 13

Holding to Life after a Storm 14

The First Meeting 15

Walling in or Walling Out 17

The Magic Carpet 18

The Desert Speaks to the Dreamer

The rooster's crowing followed the Call to Prayer,
or was the crowing first, and then the Call?
In her dove-white feathered bed, the dreamer
drowses while the two echo on top of each other
as if practiced every day to ensure perfect harmony:
One, the melodic sounds of a man, like an operatic aria
bringing the world alive to honor the Maker;
the other, sharp and urgent, like a jazz trumpet,
compelling all creatures to awaken.

Together their voices arouse the sleeper,
drawing her from unconsciousness,
lifting her from soft surroundings.
Her hands wipe the sand from her eyes.
Her tongue licks the brine from her lips.
Her feet recoil from the cold marble floor.
Pulled to the window to see the sun rising
over the desert, she leaves behind her dream of
an ocean rolling with diamond-capped waves
smashing against her body as she swims to shore.

To Calliope

Looking for you does no good.
Summoning you does not work.
No séance will bring you into this space.
You appear when you desire, to adjust,
manipulate, or expel the mundane—
perhaps—
to control the creation or the form.
Like the unseen force that keeps
opening the door I shut or
the feeling of a light touch,
brushing my calf while I sleep,
your presence is verified by what's left behind—
the door opened a hand's width each time,
my sense of not being alone while I sleep,
a dark, unknown figure emerging on the page, or
an ethereal image pushing to the surface of my work.

Darkness Lifting

The dawn was more like midnight than morning.
Thunder shook the quiet urban neighborhood.
Occasional lightning flashes broke the darkness.
Black clouds concealed the sky, allowing no light,
the sun shrouded, not existing in this world.

Suddenly, the morning became silent,
the rumblings quieted, and the clouds parted,
permitting one shaft of light like a spotlight on a stage
to shine on an egg resting in a cradle of twigs.
The nest was barely visible among waxy green leaves
of a miniature magnolia tree, beginning to bloom.

A dove alighted, settling in to protect her young,
her gray wings sheltering it from an audience of one
looking out her window at the tree and dove as the
storm cleared and sun flooded the sky with light.

The Greens of Acadia

The green surrounds, carpets the trail we walk.
The sun streaks through the leaves' tree-top abode.
The smells of pine and fir, sounds of soft talk,
like the trees whisper in a secret code,
encroaching humans cannot comprehend.
Leaves pale green of an avocado's heart
to the dark of the avocado's skin,
their diverse arras framing nature's art.

Then, deeper in, where sunlight cannot go
the other side of green emerges—decay,
algae, fungi, lichens, mold, taking hold,
spreading like veins through the body of their prey.
The Acadia forest, heaven of green,
nurtures life, death, the spiritual between.

Loss

Too many pieces
  missing,
    like a china plate
    dropped,
    pattern broken,
    symmetry shattered.
A hand reaches down,
  seeking to make it whole,
    finding only
    fragments,
    edges sharp, pointed,
    cutting, slicing the flesh,
    bringing blood,
    pain, and despair.
Until the
  not-to-be
    consumes all.

Death Waits

Death waits, not
kindly like the gentleman
in Dickinson's poem.

Instead, he hovers, lingering
until all hope's gone and
no place provides cover.

He lassos the loved every day,
leaving us to weigh our
lone being or not.

Being is surviving
despite the deep pain of
loss and despair.

Not is transcending,
merging into the spirit universal
and existing on earth no more.

Professor Lost

I heard of your death,
when my path crossed that of someone
who remembered I would care.
You died alone in a motel room surrounded
by the bottles from which you could not escape.

The first time we met,
you looked like an outdoorsman,
your face ruddy and weathered.
but your hands were pale and unmarked,
signaling they held a pen, not an axe.

Your mind, sharp as the writer
you taught us to love, you brought
Daisy Miller, Milly Theale to life.
and we admired you despite your
disappearing into darkness at times.

We learned to expect your absences
anticipating your return,
which always occurred.
Now only a lost scholar's shadow
and our memories of you remain.

The Last Word: A Sestina

What do I say now?
You always said I must have the last word,
but tonight someone else will.
My words will no longer be heard or matter.
Our chance has come and gone, and it is lost,
lost in all not said, all not done by either of us.

Moving so fast to marry shouts nothing remains for us.
Our divorce is final today, the required 30 days met now.
During the separation, I hoped our love was not forever lost.
Your marrying another creates a restless emptiness no word
can satisfy or calm. It's a deep disquiet like dark matter,
holding the galaxies together but beyond control or will.

I wonder if any future fulfillment, any means will
stop my mind from filling up with memories of us.
If we rewrite memories each remembering, can my gray matter
shift to revise you out, to quiet my thoughts, to satisfy me now,
or is despair and sorrow permanent for me? *Sorrow* is the word
most fitting to describe my feelings and regret over what is lost.

The sorrow's so deep the self of me feels lost.
No wishing alters the fact tonight you will
marry another and with you, she will have the last word.
Tonight, I am alone and soon there will be no more us.
We have destroyed what we had, forever gone now,
annihilated, like anti-matter meeting matter.

No words come to me, none that matter
or will work to touch one forever lost.
I fail to see any way to stop you now.
I cannot prevent your going to her, no will
can push her out or bring you back to make us
one again. No action will reunite us, no word.

I leave you to her and search for an evocative last word,
the right word for me alone to bring closure to the matter.
Perhaps a universal design exists, one greater than either of us,
a teleology, a purpose in the material world ensuring nothing is lost.
Maybe we are headed for something beyond our power to will
in to existence, something better, something greater now.

My last word is *hope*, the best word to push past all that's lost.
The matter that's me looks forward to new loves. It's *hope* that will
heal my heart and allow me to put us behind me forever now.

The Last Great Auk
With a Debt to Elizabeth Kolbert's Sixth Extinction

We hunted, plucked, ate, burned,
and collected you into extinction.
Audubon journeyed to Newfoundland
to paint you but arrived too late.
You and all your brethren became
extinct in the 1840s, so he used
a stuffed bird as a model for you.

In a genus unique to you,
you most resembled a Puffin.
Snow white was your chest,
silky black your back, fading
to dark gray, the same color
as your wings, too small to lift
your eleven pound body from
the ground, but there nonetheless,
perhaps forgotten in your evolutionary
development like our appendices.

You stood under three feet tall.
Your rounded, eight-inch head,
had a white trapezoid shaped spot
above your hazel eyes in summer
that molted to a white stripe
between your eyes in winter.
With webbed feet like ducks,
you preferred swimming as your
mode of transportation.

You mated for life, you and your spouse
bearing only one egg a year.
You shared egg-hatching duties,
and both cared for your young.
How heartbroken you must have been
to see your baby's fragile shell smashed
against the rocks of Eldey Island
by a monstrous human before he strangled
your love, then you, the last Great Auk.

The Lessons of Hurricanes
 To My Father

I smelled the match before I saw
the flash move toward the candle.
The light flickered and reflected in the
magical floating dust around the flame,
a flame lit by your hidden hand.
The candles held my eyes as I watched
the melting wax run down onto the plate.

You've been gone 20 years, and another
storm has come to remind me of my first.
We sat together on the red and black
checkerboard kitchen floor, waiting
to find out where that storm was going,
waiting for it to hit and for it to end.

Debra was the storm's name, my name
but you said the spelling was not right;
it should be *D-e-b-o-r-a-h* like Judge Deborah,
the only female judge in the old testament.
You, a lawyer and reader of the Bible,
chose my name to transfer her strength to me.

We gathered tall, slender white candles and
your silver flashlight in case the lights went out.
You said the storms always seem to come
in the middle of the night in the darkness.
The lights blinked and then went to sleep;
The outside darkness had come inside with us.

You said the kitchen was the safest room,
with only a small four-pane window above the sink
and a single pane window in the back door, now both
crisscrossed with tape and covered with blinds.
The counter top stood above my head, so high
it would protect us if the winds blew down trees.

The rain came in bursts, hard, then harder,
sounding like pebbles pinging against the slate roof.
The winds growled like wolves and
the tree limbs brushed against our home,
made of brick like the one that
protected the three little pigs.

A loud crash broke through
the deafening wind and the floor shook.
You went to the door window to look out.
I followed you and took your hand.
You told me to go back to the center of the room.
The neighbor's old oak tree had fallen on our garage.

Silence surrounded us—the eye had come,
still and peaceful, but deceptive in trying to fool us,
make us think the storm was over.

We waited some more,
waited until the wind and rain returned.
I rested my head on your knee and felt
your hand brushing my hair away from my face
until the candles burned out and darkness came again.

My Life on the Curb

The mountain on my curb reaches higher
than the water mark left from the flooding
that overtook my house and my life.
Piled six feet high sits my sofa, chairs,
tables, rugs, appliances, computers, TVs,
photos, and books, next to sheetrock,
wood flooring, and insulation.
All looks like trash, but it isn't.
It's my life that sits on that curb,
fifty years of memories, many from
living on this West Houston street
with its green lawns and antique oaks.
Now, the well-manicured yards are obscured
by the piles of stuff, my stuff and the stuff of
all my neighbors who, too, have lost everything.

Well-meaning helpers say, "You haven't lost *everything*.
After all, you have your life and your family."
They seek to provide some comfort and they do.
Then, I go back inside my gutted home and cry.
Gone are my family bible and other books we treasured.
Gone, too, are most of our family photos.
I tried to salvage them, but the mold
had other ideas and covered everything,
its tentacles penetrating the pores of all paper products
and all else so fast we could not stop it.
It is still growing up the remaining walls and
spreading into the sheetrock on the ceiling,
signaling to me how much more must be sacrificed
to the pile on the curb, the vestiges of my life.

Holding to Life after a Storm

Homes are gutted, turned inside out, with removed walls
and belongings covering yards from curbs to front doors,
killing grass and plants while waiting to be carried
to land fields to add to the pollution of earth.

After the wreckage is hauled away, millions of
bits of sheetrock, looking like snow, remain
scattered across the once green lawns while
children play football over the dirt and debris.

The trees stand bare, stripped of their leaves,
with limbs broken, or if toppled completely,
crossing wires or roads, until dragged to the side
of the concrete streets as decaying rubbish.

The piles of silt, natural perhaps, but
poisoned by chemicals and feculent waste
smother the natural and the manmade trails on
the once bushy banks of the bayous.

The shrimp, oysters, crabs, and fish on the shore,
are killed by the loss of the natural salinity of the Gulf,
buried in the ocean floor, or eyes glassed, floating
on the surface, beaten by the waves.

Further out, the Flower Garden Banks, a marine sanctuary
of coral reefs, home to sea turtles, mantas, sharks, and
numerous fish, face destruction from the toxic waste
of petro-chemical plants and Super Fund sites washed offshore.

The piles of debris are almost gone, and many
homes are rebuilt and refurnished, suggesting
some semblance of normal living is returning, but
nature still struggles to hold on to life after a storm.

The First Meeting
Based on My Mother-in-law Rennie's Story

The clock on the kitchen wall seemed to be watching her,
its black hands on the white face pausing in anticipation
as if it knew 1:00 would soon have a voice for the first time.
Each of her children and grandchildren had recorded
a short greeting for her at each hour, but she had left 1:00 open.
Each day as the hands of the clock made their trip around the face,
she heard each voice, except one, that of Jim, her first born.
For that hour, only silence.

She took a deep breath and looked out the front window
to glimpse Jim getting out of the car and walking to her door.
She was back over 50 years ago, 17 years-old again,
seeing an older version of Jim's father, her first love.
He looked just like him with a touch of her—
blue eyes, flushed complexion, and reddish blond hair.
All her years of looking for him had failed
yet here he came after finding her.

She glanced back at the entry hall mirror
and then, she opened the front door.
No matter how often she'd imagined this moment,
she stood frozen, unable to move or to speak.
She felt the blood move into her face.
All she could say was his name, "Jim."
They wrapped their arms around each other
and clung on as if to let go would mean
the other would vanish again.

She felt Jim's shoulders shaking,
his sobs in unison with hers.
Her baby. Now a 51-year-old man.
Where had those years gone?
All those birthdays together missed.
She had celebrated them by herself
every year since his birth,

praying for his health and
happiness wherever he was,
the baby boy she held for such a
short time before the nuns at the
New York Foundling Hospital took him away.

Why'd she let them make her give him up?
"On the streets you'll be if you keep him," her father said.
On the streets in the Bronx, a teenager with a baby.
She went back to the hospital anyway,
planning to take her baby with her,
but he had been moved to a foster home.
She went back again, but he had been adopted.
More than that the nuns would not tell her.
Her baby was gone.

Walling in or Walling Out

So disturbed by the idea of building walls,
we all should protest and shout, "No!"
History shows us the damage walls can cause:
The environment destroyed, people, too, as in
the building of the Great Wall of China,
and the Berlin Wall, a tragic symbol of
the violence it caused and families it separated.
The idea that a wall will provide protection
is as ludicrous as a demagogue who wants to build it.

Nothing is "beautiful" about a border wall,
casting foreboding shadows across the landscape.
Along the Rio Grande, it will tear up wildlife areas,
such as the National Butterfly Center and
the Santa Ana National Wildlife Refuge,
sanctuary for over 400 species of birds and plants.
Ridiculous is the idea of walling a river that meanders,
water flowing through deserts, canyons, and farm land,
as it snakes for miles, supporting wildlife and humans.

Whether walling in or walling out, walls
stop communication, hinder love, and stifle peace.
They drive wedges between the people of this earth,
when hands of all colors, sizes, genders should join as one.
A wall creates "a shield and a trap, a veil and a cage,"
Kapuscinski wrote. And Frost told us,
"Something there is that doesn't love a wall."
That something is anyone who values freedom
and the natural, open beauty of our environment.

The Magic Carpet

Where it takes you is beyond
the mundane, the ordinary.
Words emerge from notebooks or
scraps of paper or computers to be
interwoven into lines like woolen fibers
that create the ride of the imagination.

The escape into the beauty
of language elevates, clarifies, and
makes meaning deeper through
the metaphors and symbols of life.
Poetry floats above making the world
better because of its existence.

Deborah Barrett (Burch-Lavis) is a professor in the practice of writing and communication at Rice University, in Houston, where she teaches graduate courses in academic writing and research, creative writing, and literature. She has a Ph.D. in English from Rice and has published scholarly articles on literature, communication, and leadership and a textbook, *Leadership Communication* (McGraw-Hill). She has participated in the Southampton Writers Conference, the Bay Path Summer Writing Seminar in Ireland, the Iowa Summer Writing Festival, and the Bread Loaf Writers' Conferences for creative nonfiction, fiction, and poetry. She has published several creative nonfiction essays as Deborah Burch-Lavis, with her personal essay "The Last Christmas," included in the anthology *Shifts* (*Muse*Write Press), which is a 2015 USA Best Book Awards Finalist. Although she has taught the reading of poetry to undergraduate and graduate students for years and written a few poems in the past, she only recently began studying the craft of writing poetry and concentrating on improving her poetry through workshops at Bread Loaf and Stanford University. She has found a home in writing poetry and finally feels brave enough to show her poetry to others.

www.ingramcontent.com/pod-product-compliance
Lightning Source LLC
LaVergne TN
LVHW041526070426
835507LV00013B/1849